SKELETONS

An inside look at animals

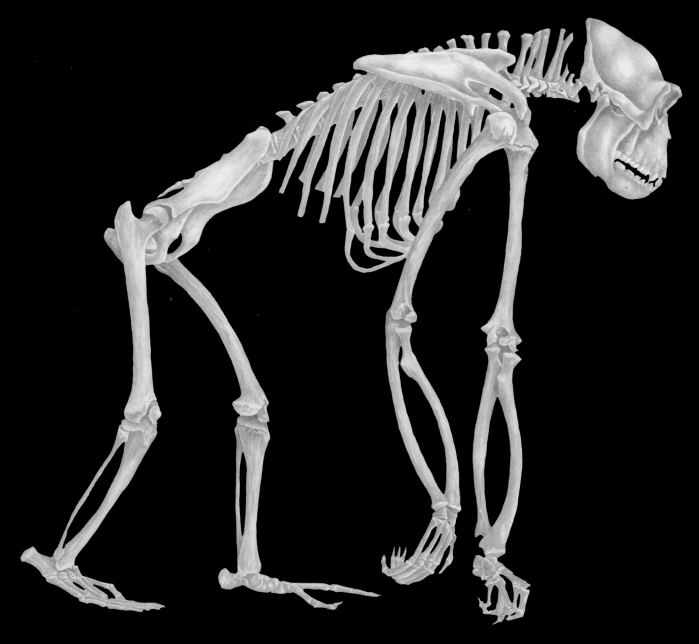

Written by
Jinny Johnson

**READER'S
DIGEST
Kids**

Illustrated by
Elizabeth Gray

Pleasantville, N.Y. • Montreal

A Reader's Digest Kids Book

Published by The Reader's Digest Association, Inc.

Copyright © 1994 Marshall Editions Developments Ltd.

Library of Congress Cataloging in Publication Data

Johnson, Jinny.
    Skeletons : an inside look at animals / Jinny Johnson ;
illustrations by Elizabeth Gray.
        p.   cm.
    ISBN 0-89577-604-9
    1. Vertebrates—Juvenile literature. 2. Bones—Juvenile
literature.   3. Skeleton—Juvenile literature.   [1. Vertebrates.
2. Bones. 3. Skeleton.]   I. Gray, Elizabeth, 1969–   i11.
II. Title.
QL605.3.J64   1994
596'.0471—dc20   94-62
                                                 CIP
                                                 AC

Produced by Marshall Editions

Executive Editor:	Cynthia O'Brien
Managing Editor:	Kate Phelps
Consultant:	Dr. Philip Whitfield
Art Director:	Branka Surla
Design Manager:	Ralph Pitchford
Research:	Jazz Wilson,
	Simon Beecroft
Editorial Director:	Ruth Binney
Production:	Barry Baker,
	Janice Storr

The editors would like to thank the Natural History
Museum, London, and the Cambridge University
Department of Zoology for their help in
the making of this book.

Printed in Italy

CONTENTS

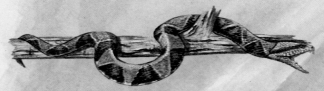

ATLANTIC COD

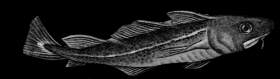

Fish were the first vertebrates—
that means animals with
backbones. The earliest fish
lived about 500 million years
ago. Since then four other groups of
vertebrate animals—amphibians,
reptiles, birds, and mammals—have
developed. All have a backbone (also
known as a spine) made up of individual
bones called vertebrae. Backbones can
be different lengths. Look at how many
vertebrae a fish has compared to the
short backbone of the frog on page 10.

All fish live in water. Some
live in salt water in the
sea, others live in
freshwater in
rivers and
lakes.

Each fin has many small bones
called fin rays. These bones keep
the fins stiff and spread out. The
bones below the fins are called
radials. They support the fins.

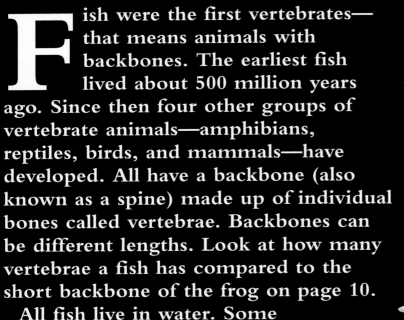

Bones
over
gills

Pectoral fins

Pelvic fins

*Like all vertebrates, fish have a bony skull
and a movable lower jaw. Special bones cover
the gills on each side of a fish's head. Gills
help a fish breathe in water. When we
breathe, our lungs absorb oxygen from the
air. When a fish breathes, oxygen is taken
out of the water as it passes through the gills.*

The three fins on the cod's back are called dorsal fins. The two fins below its body and near the tail are the ventral fins. There are also two other pairs of fins below its body. These are called the pelvic and the pectoral fins.

As the fish swims, it uses its dorsal, ventral, and tail fins to push against the water and move itself forward. It uses the pectoral and pelvic fins to help change direction.

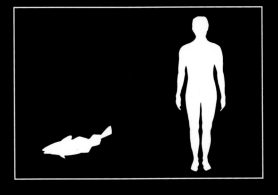

▲ A full-grown Atlantic cod is a big fish. It usually weighs about 25 pounds and is four feet long. Larger cod are rare nowadays, but fishermen sometimes see six-foot giants.

Dorsal fins

Tail fin

Ventral fins

FIERCE FISH

The cod is a fast-swimming hunter that lives in the northern Atlantic Ocean. It feeds on other fish and sea creatures such as crabs and starfish, which it catches in its sharp teeth. People like to eat cod. They catch millions of these fish every year.

FROG

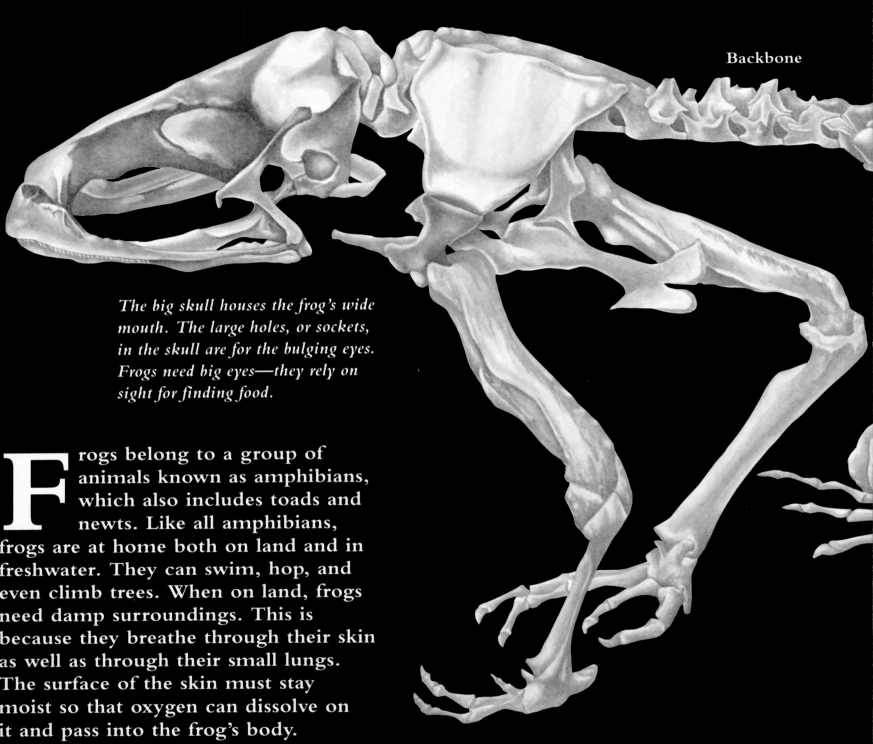

Backbone

The big skull houses the frog's wide mouth. The large holes, or sockets, in the skull are for the bulging eyes. Frogs need big eyes—they rely on sight for finding food.

Frogs belong to a group of animals known as amphibians, which also includes toads and newts. Like all amphibians, frogs are at home both on land and in freshwater. They can swim, hop, and even climb trees. When on land, frogs need damp surroundings. This is because they breathe through their skin as well as through their small lungs. The surface of the skin must stay moist so that oxygen can dissolve on it and pass into the frog's body.

Most frogs lay their eggs in water. The eggs hatch into swimming tadpoles that breathe through feathery gills at the sides of the head. As a tadpole matures, it loses its tail and gills and grows legs. About 16 weeks after hatching, the tadpole has become a tiny frog. At the top of the page, you can see how an egg changes into a leaping frog.

Foot bones

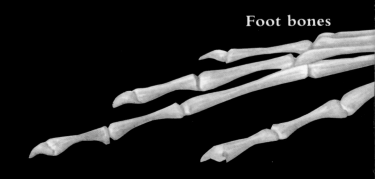

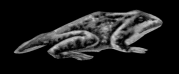  

Look at what a short backbone a frog has compared to a fish on page 8. This short spine helps to keep the frog's back rigid for jumping. The extra-long hip bones help provide power for the jump. The frog has no ribs attached to its backbone.

Hip bones

Thigh bones

Calf bones

INSECT EATER

On land, the frog eats slugs, snails, insects, and spiders. It catches its food with its long sticky tongue. As long as there is some water nearby, this frog can live happily in woodlands, fields, and even gardens.

On land, the frog crouches with its long legs folded. The foot, calf, and thigh are all about the same length. As the frog leaps, its legs unfold to push it into the air.

▶Most frogs are about four inches long—they could sit on the palm of your hand. When stretched out, a frog's back legs are usually longer than its body.

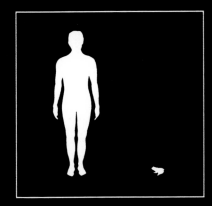

11

Green Turtle

S ea turtles spend most of their lives in the ocean, swimming with the graceful beats of their long, winglike flippers. They must come to the surface to breathe, but they can stay underwater for several hours while resting or sleeping. When turtles do come onto land, they move with difficulty, dragging themselves along with their flippers.

Turtles are reptiles like crocodiles and snakes. The green turtle is one of the biggest of the seven types of sea turtles. Like its land relative, the tortoise, the turtle has a hard shell on its back. This covers its whole body except for head, flippers, and tail. The shell is like a suit of armor, protecting the turtle from enemies. The turtle also has a shell on its underside. This is joined to the upper shell at the sides, between the turtle's front and back flippers.

Ocean Traveler

G reen turtles live in warm ocean waters throughout the world. The color of the shell varies from animal to animal. It can be olive green, dark brown, or many shades in between. Young green turtles feed on fish and shrimp. Adults eat sea grass. Green turtles are famous for the long journeys they make from their feeding places to the beaches where they lay their eggs. Turtles that live off the coast of South America travel nearly 3,000 miles to lay their eggs on tiny Ascension Island in the Atlantic Ocean.

The turtle's skull is small but strong. All the bones at the top of the head are joined together, making a protective shape like a helmet. The turtle has no teeth. It tears its food apart with its tough jaws.

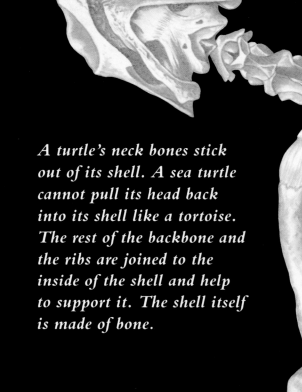

A turtle's neck bones stick out of its shell. A sea turtle cannot pull its head back into its shell like a tortoise. The rest of the backbone and the ribs are joined to the inside of the shell and help to support it. The shell itself is made of bone.

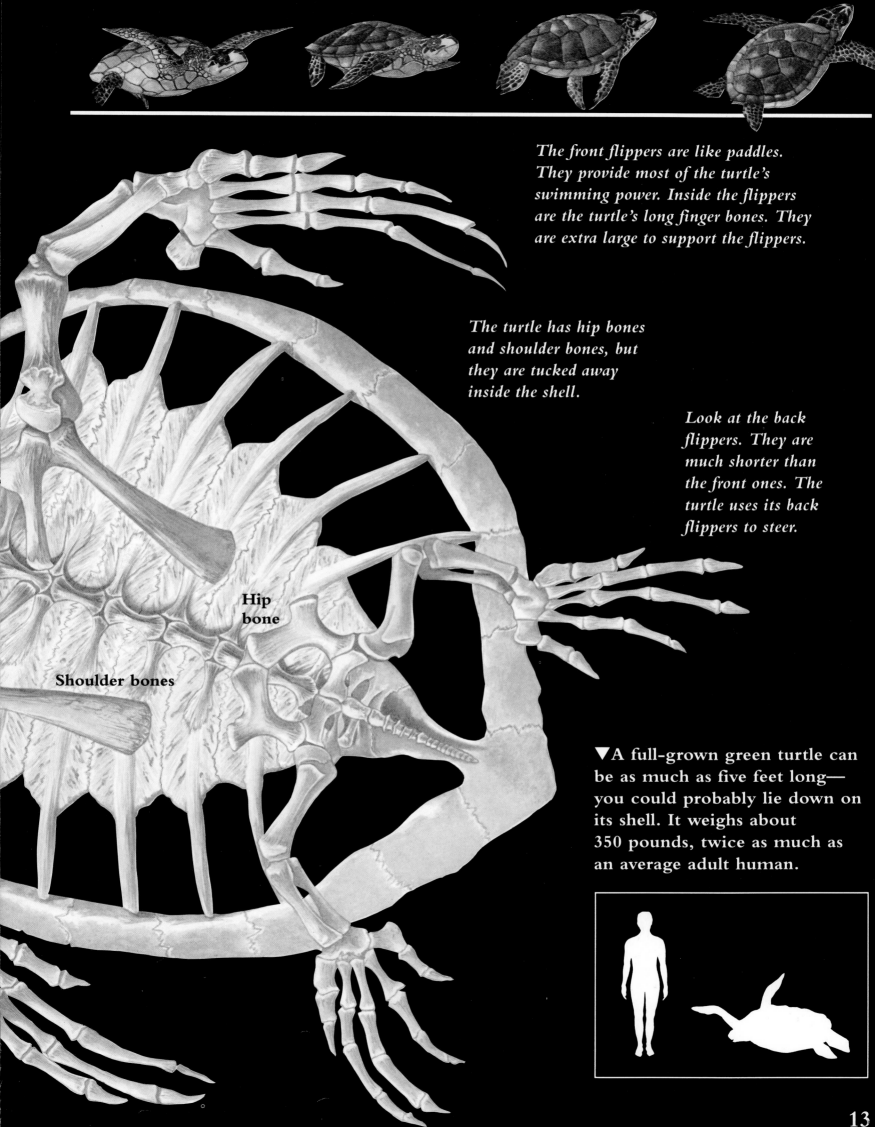

The front flippers are like paddles. They provide most of the turtle's swimming power. Inside the flippers are the turtle's long finger bones. They are extra large to support the flippers.

The turtle has hip bones and shoulder bones, but they are tucked away inside the shell.

Look at the back flippers. They are much shorter than the front ones. The turtle uses its back flippers to steer.

Hip bone

Shoulder bones

▼A full-grown green turtle can be as much as five feet long— you could probably lie down on its shell. It weighs about 350 pounds, twice as much as an average adult human.

NILE CROCODILE

Crocodiles have not changed a great deal since prehistoric times. They still look almost the same as the first crocodiles which lived at the time of the dinosaurs, 200 million years ago. Crocodiles are among the largest of all reptiles. They are related to the alligator, the caiman, and the gavial—a crocodile with a long thin snout.

Crocodiles and alligators are at home both on land and in water and are excellent swimmers. They have long bodies, strong tails, and short legs. An armor of thick scales covers the body and is made even stronger on the back by pieces of bone under the scales.

All crocodiles are meat-eaters and hunt for their food. They often lurk half-hidden in a river or waterhole, waiting for prey to come near. With surprising speed, they then seize the victim in their long jaws.

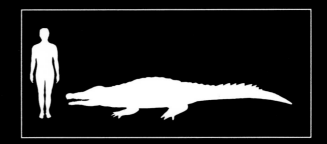

▲ From its nose to the tip of its tail, a Nile crocodile measures about 16 feet—longer than most cars.

Look at the eye sockets at the top of the head and the nostrils at the end of the top jaw. The crocodile's eyes and nose are often all that can be seen as it lies in the water watching for prey.

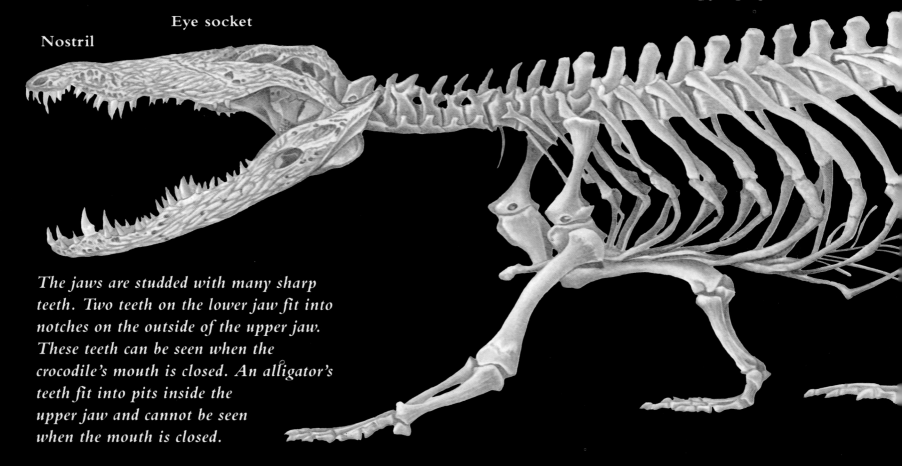

Eye socket

Nostril

The jaws are studded with many sharp teeth. Two teeth on the lower jaw fit into notches on the outside of the upper jaw. These teeth can be seen when the crocodile's mouth is closed. An alligator's teeth fit into pits inside the upper jaw and cannot be seen when the mouth is closed.

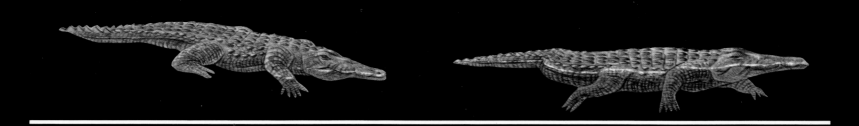

DEADLY AMBUSHER

The Nile crocodile is a fierce hunter. It lives in and alongside rivers, lakes, and waterholes in Africa. Young crocodiles eat small creatures such as insects and frogs. But full-grown crocodiles ambush animals as large as zebra and buffalo.

A crocodile can move on land in two ways. It can wriggle along on its belly, pushing itself with its feet (see above). Or it can raise itself off the ground in what is called the "high walk" (see skeleton). A crocodile has five toes on each front foot and four on each back foot.

A long spine and strong tail make the crocodile's body flexible and help it to move in water. The crocodile swims by waving its tail from side to side. As it swims, it holds its legs close to its body. This streamlines the crocodile's shape so that it can move through the water faster.

15

PIT VIPER

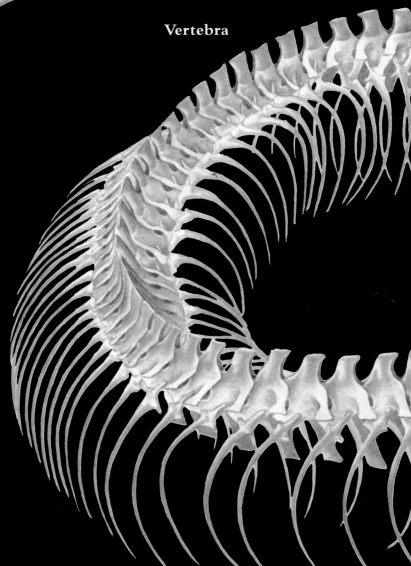

Even though they have no legs, snakes can move fast. Besides wriggling along the ground, most also swim well and can even climb trees. Along with crocodiles and turtles, snakes belong to the group of animals called reptiles. There are more than two thousand types of snakes—from four-inch-long thread snakes to 30-foot pythons. Snakes live in most places in the world except where it is very cold.

All snakes hunt other animals for food. Some, such as the boas, are constrictors. They wrap victims in their strong body coils and squeeze them to death. Others, such as cobras and vipers, have a deadly poisonous bite.

The snake's lightweight skull is made up mostly of jaw bones. This animal can open its mouth very wide because its upper and lower jaws are loosely joined. This allows the snake to swallow large prey.

Vertebra

NIGHTTIME HUNTER

This dangerous pit viper lives in the forests of Central and South America. It can hunt in the dark with amazing accuracy. On each side of its head is a small pit which is sensitive to heat. When an animal comes near, the snake senses its body heat with these pits and knows just where to strike.

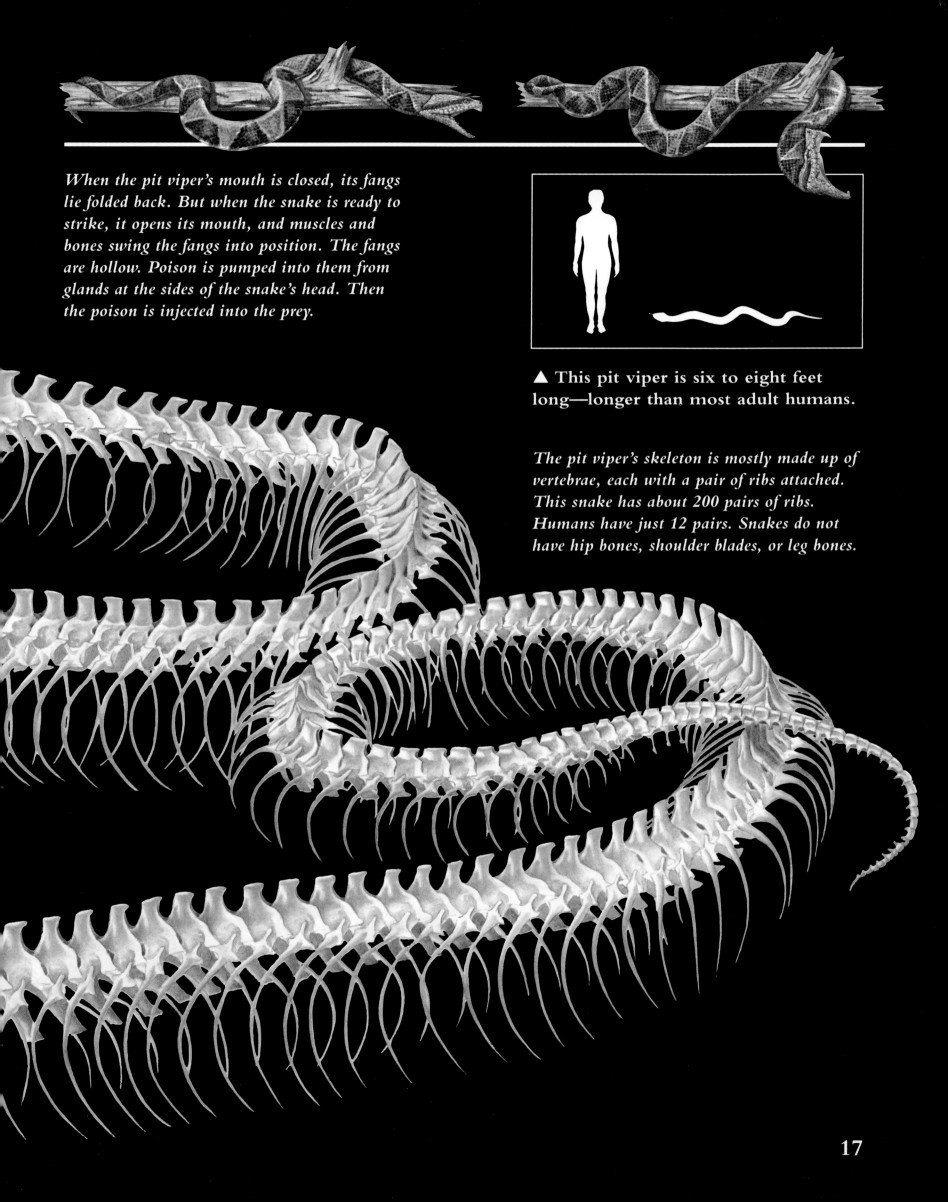

When the pit viper's mouth is closed, its fangs lie folded back. But when the snake is ready to strike, it opens its mouth, and muscles and bones swing the fangs into position. The fangs are hollow. Poison is pumped into them from glands at the sides of the snake's head. Then the poison is injected into the prey.

▲ This pit viper is six to eight feet long—longer than most adult humans.

The pit viper's skeleton is mostly made up of vertebrae, each with a pair of ribs attached. This snake has about 200 pairs of ribs. Humans have just 12 pairs. Snakes do not have hip bones, shoulder blades, or leg bones.

17

SCARLET MACAW

The skull is light so it does not weigh the bird down in the air. There are large spaces for the macaw's big eyes.

Nostril

Beak

A bird flaps its wings with the help of large muscles. These are attached to a big, triangular bone called a keel. The keel is part of the bird's sternum (or breastbone).

Like all birds, the macaw has no teeth. Instead it has a big hooked beak which covers much of its top and bottom jaws. The beak is made of the same hard material as our finger and toe nails. The two halves of the beak can clamp together to crush food—just like a strong nutcracker.

Breastbone

Keel

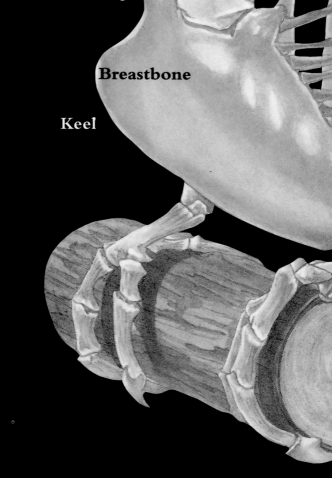

There are more than 9,000 species of birds in the world. All have feathers, and most can fly. Birds lay eggs which they usually keep warm in nests until their young hatch.

The scarlet macaw is a species of parrot. It is one of the biggest birds in the parrot family, which also includes cockatoos, parakeets, and lovebirds. Parrots are found in the southern half of the world in South America, Africa, Asia, and Australia. They usually live in rainforests or woodlands where they find plenty of fruit, seeds, and nuts to eat. Their strong beaks can crack the hardest shells.

Many kinds of macaws are so beautiful that they have become popular pets. Sadly, this means that some are now very rare in nature. In most countries, it is against the law to take rare birds from the wild to keep as pets.

A bird's bones are not as solid as ours. They are like a honeycomb inside; spaces filled with air keep them light. It would be hard for a bird with heavy bones to fly.

A bird's wing has arm and finger bones similar to those of land animals. But each wing has only three finger bones. The main flying feathers—called the primaries—are attached to the arm bones and the two long finger bones. A third short finger bone supports a "mini-wing" in front of the main wing. This mini-wing helps control the air flow over the main wing.

SCARLET BEAUTY

With its brilliant red and blue feathers, the scarlet macaw is one of the most striking birds. It usually lives in pairs or families that fly together, searching for nuts and seeds. Scarlet macaws feed quietly but make loud screeching cries when flying. They build nests in holes in tree trunks and lay two or three eggs.

Finger bones

Tail bone

"Mini-wing" bone

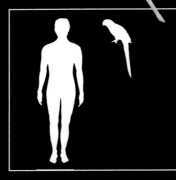

Each foot has four toes—two pointing forward, two backward. (Many other birds have three toes pointing forward and one backward.) The macaw's foot is like a clamp—ideal for gripping branches.

◀ The scarlet macaw is about 33 inches long from its head to the tip of its long tail feathers.

CAPE PENGUIN

Unlike most birds, penguins can't fly. They use their wings like flippers to swim. There are 18 different kinds of penguins. All have mostly black feathers on their backs and white on their stomachs. This coloration helps keep them hidden from enemies in the water.

Penguins live in the oceans of the southern hemisphere, mainly around the icy continent of Antarctica. They spend nearly all of their lives in the sea where they catch fish and squid to eat. The fastest penguin is the gentoo which swims at more than six miles an hour for short distances—faster than the best human swimmers, who are three times its size.

Penguins come onto land to lay their eggs and care for their young. They waddle around upright on their short legs. On ice they sometimes toboggan along, lying flat on their bellies.

The penguin's wings are shaped for swimming instead of flying. They are smaller than the wings of other birds this size and cannot be folded back against the body. The bones are flattened to form a paddle-like shape.

The penguin has more tail bones than the scarlet macaw (see page 19). These bones keep the tail stiff so it can prop the penguin up when it stands on land.

Front toes

The penguin uses its feet for steering. There are three long front toes, all with strong claws, and a very small fourth toe which is joined to the ankle bone. A web of skin connects the front toes and makes them into more efficient paddles.

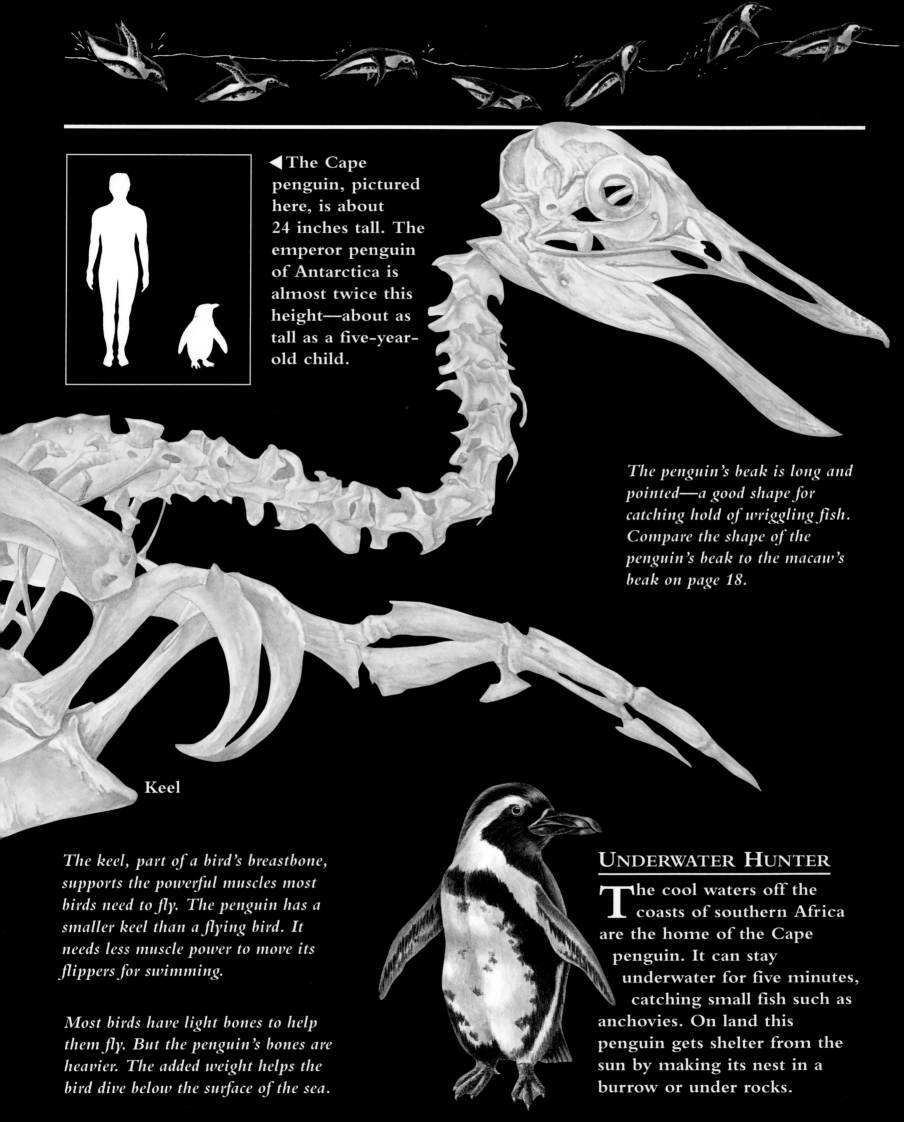

◄The Cape penguin, pictured here, is about 24 inches tall. The emperor penguin of Antarctica is almost twice this height—about as tall as a five-year-old child.

The penguin's beak is long and pointed—a good shape for catching hold of wriggling fish. Compare the shape of the penguin's beak to the macaw's beak on page 18.

Keel

The keel, part of a bird's breastbone, supports the powerful muscles most birds need to fly. The penguin has a smaller keel than a flying bird. It needs less muscle power to move its flippers for swimming.

Most birds have light bones to help them fly. But the penguin's bones are heavier. The added weight helps the bird dive below the surface of the sea.

UNDERWATER HUNTER

The cool waters off the coasts of southern Africa are the home of the Cape penguin. It can stay underwater for five minutes, catching small fish such as anchovies. On land this penguin gets shelter from the sun by making its nest in a burrow or under rocks.

RED KANGAROO

Big and bounding, kangaroos belong to a group of mammals known as marsupials. The word marsupial means pouched animal. Most marsupials have a pouch like a furry pocket in which their young grow and develop. The marsupial baby is born less developed than the babies of other mammals. Immediately after birth, the tiny baby crawls into its mother's pouch. Here it feeds on its mother's milk and grows in safety.

There are more than 250 kinds of marsupials, including marsupial cats and mice, bandicoots, and koalas. Most of these live in Australia and nearby New Guinea, but many kinds of opossums live in North and South America.

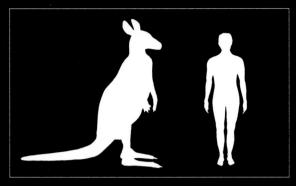

▲ Red kangaroos are the largest kangaroos—and the biggest marsupials. A male stands taller than many adult humans. Its head and body are more than five feet long and its tail measures at least three feet.

DESERT LEAPER

Kangaroos can move on all four legs, but they usually leap along on their strong back legs like the kangaroo at the top of the page. Red kangaroos live in the vast Australian desert and need to travel huge distances to find enough grass and leaves to eat.

When a baby kangaroo is born, it is no bigger than an adult human's thumb. It stays in its mother's pouch until it is over a year old and big enough to find its own food.

A kangaroo's long tail is extremely strong. Look at how big the bones are. Powerful muscles for moving the tail are attached to bones called neural spines. These stick out from the tail bones. The kangaroo uses its tail for balance when it hops. The tail also props up the kangaroo when it stands on its back legs.

Neural spines

The long backbone is strong but flexible enough to bend and straighten as the kangaroo hops along. Look at the pictures above to see how the backbone moves. The red kangaroo can run at a speed of up to 40 miles an hour. That's a good speed for a car. It can also jump as high as ten feet—twice its own height.

The kangaroo's skull is long and fairly flat on top. The teeth at the front of the long jaws are for chopping off mouthfuls of leaves or grass. Then the tongue moves the food to the teeth farther back in the jaws where it is ground down before swallowing.

Shin bone

The back legs are much longer than the front legs. The shin bone, or tibia, is especially large. The powerful leg muscles are attached to this bone. The large back feet have four toes. The one long toe is used for jumping and walking, and the smaller ones for grooming the fur.

The kangaroo uses its shorter front legs to move on all fours or to hold food. There are sharp claws on the tips of the five long fingers. Rival males fighting over mates sometimes use these claws as weapons when they "box" with one another.

FRUIT BAT

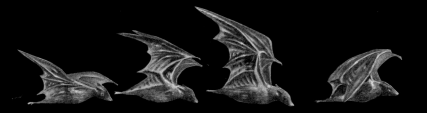

Bats take to the sky when night falls. They are mammals like cats, dogs, monkeys, and humans, but bats can fly just as well as birds. They have wings made of thin skin, supported by the long bones of their arms and "hands." The bones are light so the bats are not too heavy to fly. Bats cannot move easily on land. They crawl along, using their back feet and the claws at the tips of their wings.

During the day fruit bats sleep in groups of thousands, hanging upside down in caves or from the branches of trees. Many bats eat insects, but fruit bats eat soft fruits such as figs. Their keen sense of smell helps them find the ripest fruit.

Claw

All bats have a claw on their first finger. Fruit bats also have a claw on each second finger. They use their claws to climb in trees and to hold food.

"Finger" bones

These long bones are the finger bones of the bat's "hands." They help support the wings which stretch down the sides of the body and legs and across to the tips of the fingers. Look at the bird skeleton on page 18, and see how different its wing bones are from those of the bat.

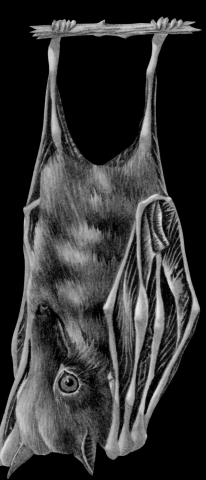

FLYING FOX

There are more than 170 types of fruit bat. They are often called flying foxes because of their foxlike faces. Fruit bats live in tropical places like Southeast Asia and northern Australia where there is always plenty of ripe fruit to feed on. Like all bats, the fruit bat folds its wings close to its sides and hangs by its feet when it rests.

Fruit bats have excellent eyesight. Look at the size of the sockets that house the large eyes of these night animals.

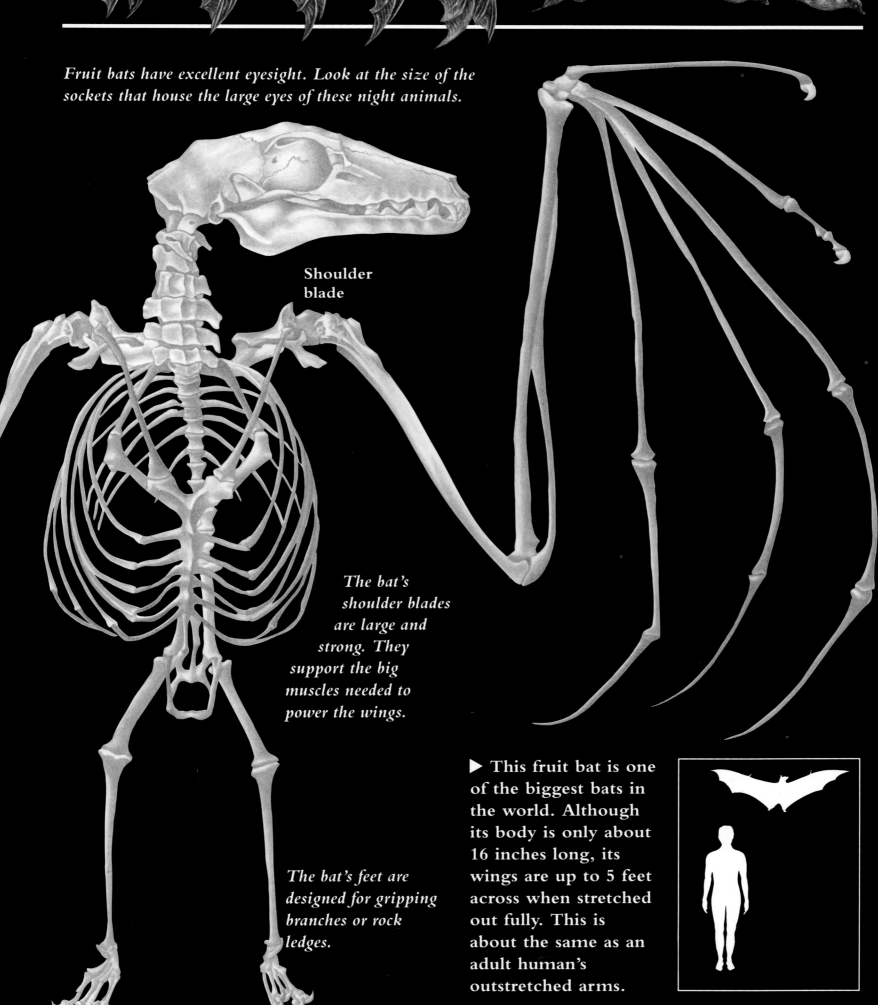

Shoulder blade

The bat's shoulder blades are large and strong. They support the big muscles needed to power the wings.

The bat's feet are designed for gripping branches or rock ledges.

▶ This fruit bat is one of the biggest bats in the world. Although its body is only about 16 inches long, its wings are up to 5 feet across when stretched out fully. This is about the same as an adult human's outstretched arms.

LION

The lion has a short, rounded skull with strong jaws. Huge muscles are attached to the big bony ridge at the back of the skull. These help the lion snap its jaws shut in a killer bite.

The lion kills its prey with the daggerlike teeth, called canines, at the front of its jaws.

The mighty lion with its ferocious roar is actually a big cat. The cat family includes about 37 species, ranging from small wild cats and domestic cats to large, powerful tigers and lions.

Aside from their size, all cats are quite similar. They are hunters that catch other animals with their sharp teeth and claws. They follow their prey quietly or lie in wait. Then they pounce—just like the lion at the top of the page. Lions have excellent eyesight. They see much better in the dark than humans. Their good hearing helps them track down prey.

A male lion has a thick collar of hair called a mane on his neck. It makes him appear larger than he is and more threatening. A female lion is called a lioness and does not have a mane.

The lion has sharp curved claws on its feet. Each claw folds back onto the bone behind it and is protected by the fleshy paw. The claws are kept out of the way when not needed so their points stay sharp.

The backbone bends easily so the lion can crouch low and slink along the ground when it stalks its prey.

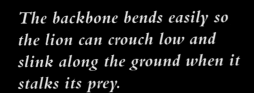

CARING MOTHER

Most lions live in Africa, but some roam a small area of northern India. Unlike most cats, lions live in families called prides. A pride includes as many as 18 animals, mostly females and young.

Lionesses are good mothers. They care for their cubs for up to two years and teach them how to hunt.

When a lion runs, its long tail swings from side to side. This helps the lion keep its balance.

▼ **A full-grown lion is big and heavy. It is eight to ten feet long, and its tail adds another three feet. A male lion weighs about 450 pounds—as much as three human adults. A lioness is slightly smaller and lighter.**

Long slender legs help the lion move fast. Lions can run at a speed of more than 35 miles an hour but only for short distances.

ELEPHANT SEAL

The mighty elephant seal is the biggest of all seals. Its huge body is covered with a thick layer of fatty blubber to protect it from the cold. It weighs as much as a full-grown rhinoceros.

Like sealions and walruses, seals are mammals. They are descended from the same land creatures as cats and dogs but spend most of their time in the sea. Their bodies are torpedo-shaped to suit their watery lives. Instead of legs, they have flippers which they use to move on land and in the sea.

All seals come out of the water to mate and to give birth. Once a year, huge numbers of elephant seals gather together on beaches. Males fight one another to win control of sections of the beach. The winners can mate with the females in their areas. Rival males rear up facing one another; then they crash their great bodies together like the elephant seals at the top of the page. The male elephant seal has a big fleshy snout, which it can puff up when threatening a rival.

The long toe bones of the back feet support the flippers. These flippers provide most of the elephant seal's swimming power.

DEEP DIVER

Elephant seals live along the west coast of North America and around the icy coasts of Antarctica. They can dive down as deep as 1,000 feet to catch fish and squid.

Thigh bone

Lower leg bone

The seal's leg bones are like those of land animals, but they are extremely short and are contained mostly within the body. Compare the short thigh bone, or femur, of the seal to the thigh bone of the horse on page 37 .

Toe bones

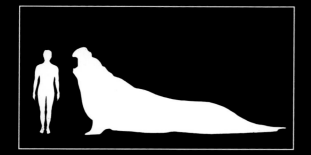

◄ A male elephant seal weighs about 5,000 pounds— more than 30 adult humans. A female weighs less than half as much.

The elephant seal's backbone is very flexible so that the animal can move easily in water. The vertebrae at the end of the backbone are especially big and strong. They support the large muscles needed to move the seal's hind flippers.

At the front of the elephant seal's heavy jaws are sharp pointed teeth called canines. The seal snaps up slippery prey, such as fish, with these. Then it chews its food with the rounded teeth farther back.

The front flippers of the elephant seal contain short, thick leg bones and long finger bones. The seal can prop itself up on these flippers when on land. When swimming, it usually holds these front flippers close to its body so they are out of the way.

Each of the elephant seal's main ribs is divided into two parts. The top part is made of bone, and the bottom part is made of a tough, springy material called cartilage. When the seal dives, the water presses on its chest. The flexible cartilage allows the chest to cave in under this pressure without crushing the ribs.

BLUE WHALE

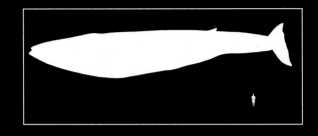

Whales are mammals like cats, dogs, and humans, but they spend their lives swimming in the ocean. They are even born underwater. A whale has a streamlined body like a fish, and flippers instead of legs. Nonetheless, whales need air, so they must come to the water's surface to breathe.

There are two kinds of whales—toothed whales and baleen whales. Toothed whales include killer whales, dolphins, and porpoises. They have sharp teeth and hunt for prey such as fish and penguins. Baleen whales, such as the humpback and the blue whale, are the real giants. Instead of teeth, these whales have huge chunks of a thick, hairy material called baleen hanging from their top jaws. To feed, a baleen whale opens its mouth, and water flows in. Shrimp and other tiny creatures get caught on the baleen, which acts like a sieve. Then the whale swallows the food.

▲ The blue whale is the biggest animal that has ever lived on Earth. It is up to 100 feet long and weighs about 130 tons— more than 80 cars!

The whale has a very short neck, with bones close together. This short neck keeps the body streamlined. If the whale had a long neck, its head would flop around in the water.

The blowhole at the top of the head is the whale's nostril. It allows the whale to breathe without taking its head completely out of the water.

Blowhole

Because the whale's jaw bones are long and curved, there's plenty of room for the bristly baleen.

A whale's front flippers and a land animal's front legs have the same type of main bones. The "fingers" supporting the flippers are long. Most mammals have three bones in each finger. Blue whales have as many as eight.

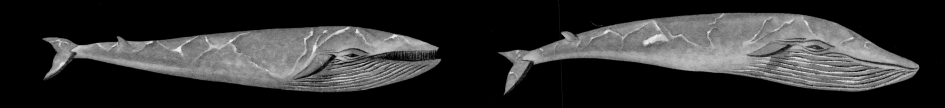

OCEAN GIANT

Blue whales spend some of the year in the icy Arctic and Antarctic oceans where there are plenty of tiny shrimp to eat. In winter they move to warmer waters where the females have their babies. Even a baby blue whale is huge. When it is born, it is about 22 feet long. It would stretch across the floor of a large room. The baby drinks about 150 gallons of its mother's rich milk a day and doubles its weight in a week.

A whale skeleton is surprisingly light. The water supports the whale's weight so its skeleton does not need to be very strong. The skeleton of a land animal of the same size would need to be much heavier.

A whale moves its tail up and down to push itself through the water. Big muscles for moving the tail are attached to the spines sticking out from the tail bones.

Tail bones

Some whales have hip and back leg bones. This means they are related to creatures that walk on land. The blue whale has tiny hip bones that are not joined to the rest of the skeleton.

Hip bones

31

AFRICAN ELEPHANT

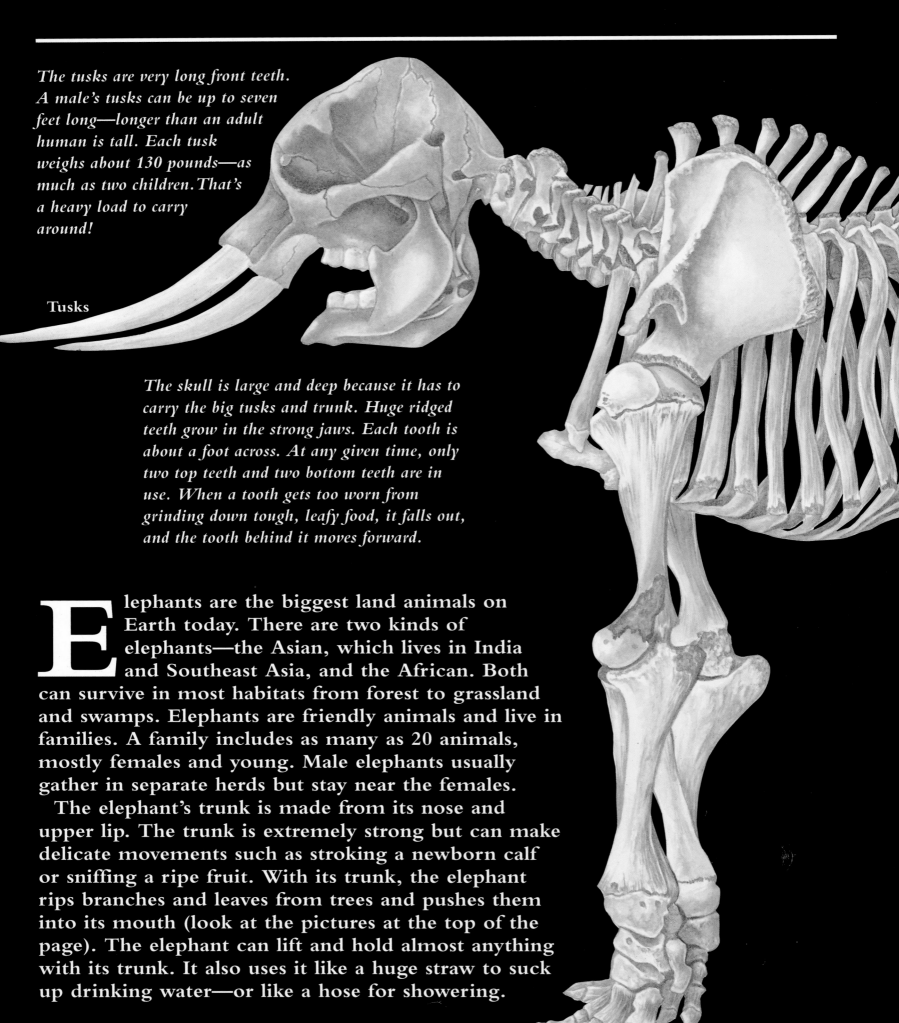

The tusks are very long front teeth. A male's tusks can be up to seven feet long—longer than an adult human is tall. Each tusk weighs about 130 pounds—as much as two children. That's a heavy load to carry around!

Tusks

The skull is large and deep because it has to carry the big tusks and trunk. Huge ridged teeth grow in the strong jaws. Each tooth is about a foot across. At any given time, only two top teeth and two bottom teeth are in use. When a tooth gets too worn from grinding down tough, leafy food, it falls out, and the tooth behind it moves forward.

Elephants are the biggest land animals on Earth today. There are two kinds of elephants—the Asian, which lives in India and Southeast Asia, and the African. Both can survive in most habitats from forest to grassland and swamps. Elephants are friendly animals and live in families. A family includes as many as 20 animals, mostly females and young. Male elephants usually gather in separate herds but stay near the females.

The elephant's trunk is made from its nose and upper lip. The trunk is extremely strong but can make delicate movements such as stroking a newborn calf or sniffing a ripe fruit. With its trunk, the elephant rips branches and leaves from trees and pushes them into its mouth (look at the pictures at the top of the page). The elephant can lift and hold almost anything with its trunk. It also uses it like a huge straw to suck up drinking water—or like a hose for showering.

The thick backbone is unusually straight and inflexible. There are about 20 large ribs. An elephant cannot bend over. It has to kneel down or reach with its trunk.

▲ A male African elephant can be 12 feet tall and more than 24 feet long. It weighs around 13,000 pounds. Just one elephant can weigh more than 200 children.

The elephant's leg bones need to be thick and heavy to carry its massive body.

BIG EATER

E ven a baby African elephant is heavier than most adult humans. A newborn baby weighs about 240 pounds. Elephants eat leaves, twigs, bark, fruit, and roots. They need about 400 pounds of food a day. Imagine eating 400 lettuces or 1,000 apples!

An elephant has big, broad feet. There are five toes on each foot, tipped with nails like tiny hooves. At the back of each foot is a thick, springy pad of skin. It helps to cushion and spread the animal's weight.

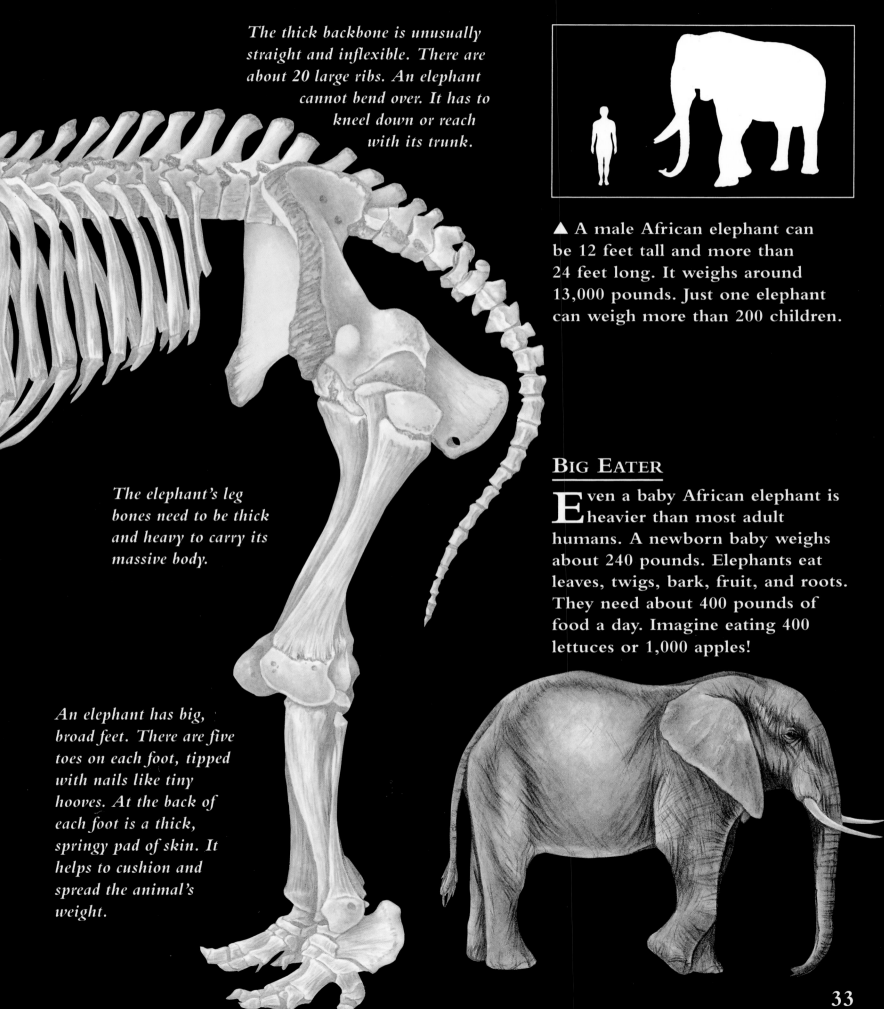

33

MOOSE

Antlers

The bones sticking up from the backbone are called neural spines. They are attached to powerful muscles. These muscles stretch to the back of the heavy head and help to support it.

Neural spines

Antlers are made of bone and grow from the top of the skull. Each winter, after the mating season, the moose's antlers drop off. A new pair grows with more branches than those of the year before. Antlers grow fast—more than half an inch a day.

Outside toes

With its huge, spreading antlers and humped shoulders, the moose is an awesome creature. It is the largest member of the deer family. There are more than 30 kinds of deer, including the caribou (or reindeer), the white-tailed deer, and the tiny musk deer which weighs only 20 pounds.

Most male deer have antlers. Females, except for female caribou, do not. Male deer use their antlers in fierce battles with rival males to win mates. They push each other back and forth, snorting and grunting, until one of them gives in and goes away—as is shown at the top of the page.

34

WOODLAND DWELLER

Moose live in wooded areas in North America. In summer they eat mostly the water weeds in ponds. In winter they feed on twigs and tree bark.

Trees are useful to moose in another way. When new antlers first grow in, they are covered with soft skin called velvet. This skin carries blood to the growing antlers. Once the antlers are full grown, the velvet starts to fall off. The moose rubs its antlers against a tree to remove the last shreds. Otherwise the velvet might get in the moose's way when it fights.

Knee

Ankle

Middle toes

The moose walks around on its toes. Just look at where its ankles are! The bones below the ankle look like part of the leg, but they are actually long foot bones.

Like all deer, the moose has four toes on each foot. The ancestors of the moose walked with all four toes on the ground. But as the moose evolved, its feet changed to help make it a fast runner. The two large middle toes form the hoof that the moose walks on. The two outside toes are much smaller and are no longer used for walking.

▼ A male moose is more than eight feet long and stands up to six feet high at the shoulder. With its mighty antlers, it towers over humans. Female moose are smaller—about three-quarters the size of males.

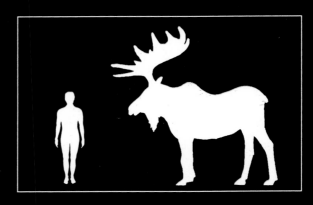

HORSE

For more than five thousand years, horses have worked for humans. Before cars and trains were invented, horses were a main form of transport. They carried loads and people and pulled farm equipment. There are still working horses on farms and ranches, and millions are also used for racing, riding, and other sports.

Horses belong to the group of mammals that also includes donkeys and zebras. Tame (or domestic) horses are found all over the world. Today the only true wild species is the Przewalski's horse of Asia.

Horses have four different ways of moving—walking, trotting, cantering, and, fastest of all, galloping. The horse at the top of the page is galloping. At one stage of the gallop, all four feet are off the ground.

The horse has a long narrow skull. The many teeth it needs for chewing grass can fit inside its big jaws. Look at how large the nostril area is. Horses have a very good sense of smell.

The big teeth at the front of the jaws are called incisors. The horse uses these to chop off mouthfuls of grass. Then the horse chews up its food with the molar teeth farther back.

GRASS EATER

Domestic horses like this one often work hard, carrying loads or racing. They are given plenty of different grains, such as oats and barley, to eat—as well as grass and hay. In the wild, horses eat grass and other small plants. They spend most of their day feeding.

Bones called neural spines stick up from the horse's backbone. Strong muscles to lift the heavy head and neck are attached to these. The big rib cage protects the lungs. A horse has large lungs so that it can take in lots of air as it runs fast.

▶ The average domestic horse stands between five and six feet high from hoof to shoulder—taller than most humans. It weighs about 1,300 pounds—as much as eight or nine adult humans.

The horse can flick its tail over its back to brush away irritating insects. The muscles that move the tail are attached to the spines at the top of the tail.

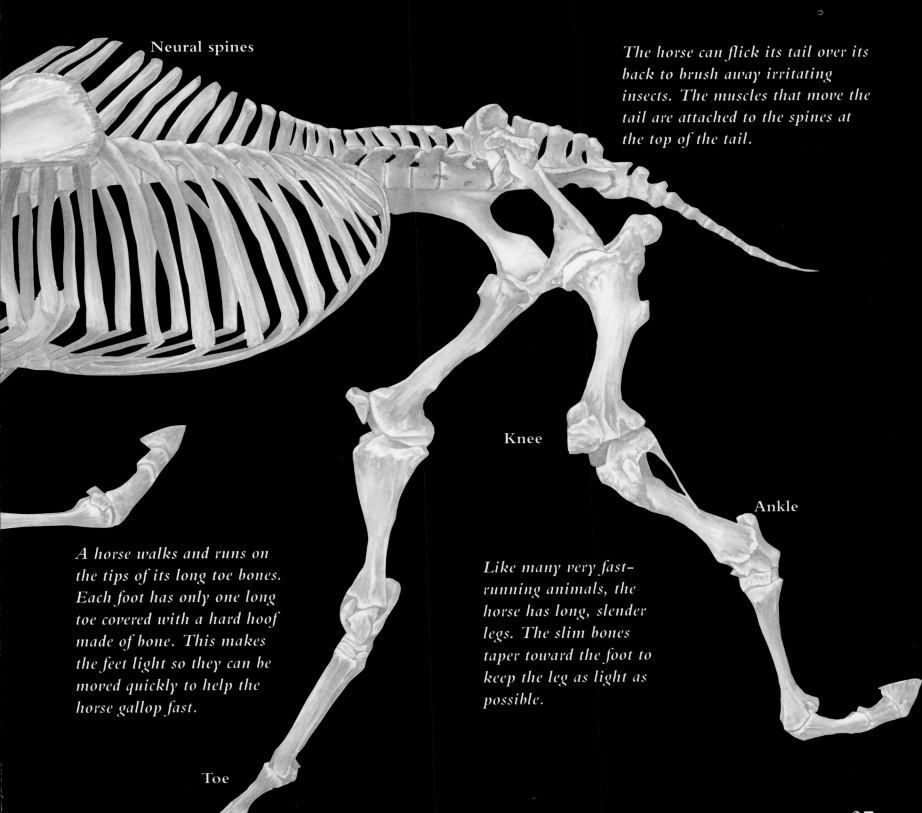

Neural spines

Knee

Ankle

A horse walks and runs on the tips of its long toe bones. Each foot has only one long toe covered with a hard hoof made of bone. This makes the feet light so they can be moved quickly to help the horse gallop fast.

Like many very fast-running animals, the horse has long, slender legs. The slim bones taper toward the foot to keep the leg as light as possible.

Toe

37

THREE-TOED SLOTH

Sloths are famous for moving slowly. One mother sloth "hurrying" to her baby took an hour to travel 15 feet! These strange mammals spend much of their lives hanging upside down in trees in South American rainforests. They rarely come down to the ground. Sloths have become so adapted to their upside-down life that they can no longer stand upright on land. They can only drag themselves along with their long front legs. But sloths are good swimmers and can move easily in jungle rivers.

There are two different types of sloths—three-toed and two-toed. All sloths have three toes on their back feet, but two-toed sloths have only two on their front feet. Sloths feed mostly on leaves. Their sight is poor, so they find their food by smell and touch. A sloth's stomach works as slowly as its legs. It can take up to a month to digest a meal.

◀ The three-toed sloth is about two feet long including its short tail. It weighs about nine or ten pounds—not much more than a large domestic cat.

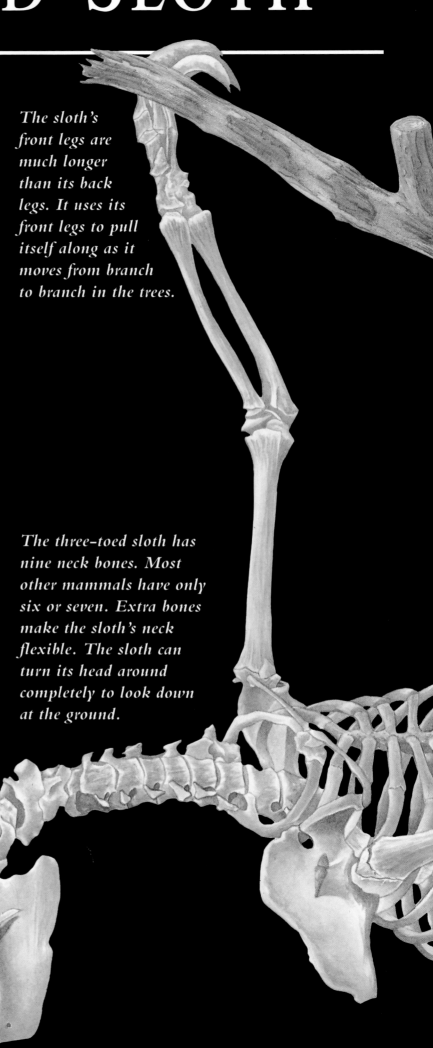

The sloth's front legs are much longer than its back legs. It uses its front legs to pull itself along as it moves from branch to branch in the trees.

The three-toed sloth has nine neck bones. Most other mammals have only six or seven. Extra bones make the sloth's neck flexible. The sloth can turn its head around completely to look down at the ground.

The sloth's skull is short and rounded. It has 16 to 20 teeth which get worn down from chewing tough leaves.

A strong claw—about three inches long—tips each toe. These claws are like hooks which the sloth uses to hang onto branches. The sloth clings so tightly that it can even sleep upside down!

Claws

UPSIDE-DOWN CLIMBER

The sloth is well-suited for upside-down life. Its fur even grows differently from that of most animals. Hairs grow down from the stomach to the backbone. This means that rain can run off the fur when the sloth is hanging upside down.

The sloth's fur is often so damp that tiny plants called algae grow in grooves in the hairs. The algae, which look like green slime, give the sloth's fur a greenish tint. The color helps the sloth hide from enemies such as harpy eagles and jaguars.

GORILLA

Gorillas may look fierce, but these great apes are usually peaceful, gentle creatures. They belong to the group of mammals known as primates that also includes chimpanzees and humans.

Gorillas live in dense tropical rainforests in central and west Africa. They spend most of the day feeding on plants such as bamboo, thistles, and vines. Some gorillas also eat insects, slugs, and snails. At night they curl up in nests made of branches and leaves up in the trees or down on the ground.

Gorillas can walk on two legs, but they usually move around on all fours. They are good climbers. Gorillas rarely fight, but if two dominant males meet, or if a young male intrudes on another male's family, they often rear up, beat their chests, and roar to threaten one another.

FAMILY DWELLER

Gorillas live in families made up of mothers and young led by an older male. Most families have ten or twelve members, but some have up to 30. The male leaders are called silverbacks because silvery white hair grows on their backs after the age of ten or so. Young males live alone for some years after leaving their parents and before they have their own families.

The front of the gorilla's skull comes forward to form a snout. It is not flat like a human face. A bony ridge on the forehead helps protect the eyes from injury.

The gorilla's arms are longer than its legs. When it moves on all fours, the gorilla leans on the knuckles of its hands.

Knuckles

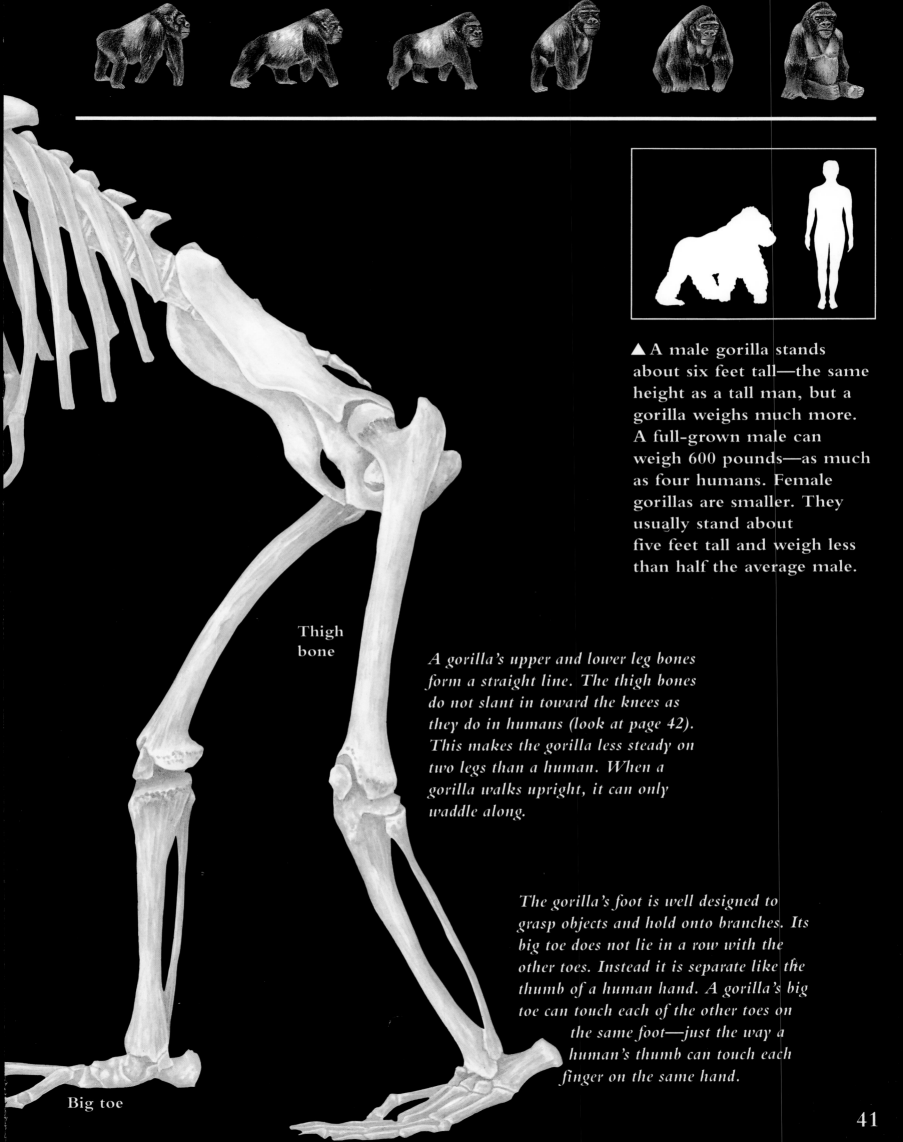

▲ A male gorilla stands about six feet tall—the same height as a tall man, but a gorilla weighs much more. A full-grown male can weigh 600 pounds—as much as four humans. Female gorillas are smaller. They usually stand about five feet tall and weigh less than half the average male.

Thigh bone

A gorilla's upper and lower leg bones form a straight line. The thigh bones do not slant in toward the knees as they do in humans (look at page 42). This makes the gorilla less steady on two legs than a human. When a gorilla walks upright, it can only waddle along.

The gorilla's foot is well designed to grasp objects and hold onto branches. Its big toe does not lie in a row with the other toes. Instead it is separate like the thumb of a human hand. A gorilla's big toe can touch each of the other toes on the same foot—just the way a human's thumb can touch each finger on the same hand.

Big toe

41

HUMAN

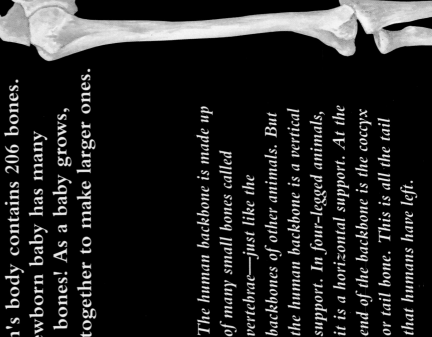

Scientists believe that the first humans evolved about two million years ago. Today there are more than five billion humans, and we rule life on Earth. But we have a long way to go to beat the dinosaurs' record. They were the dominant animals on the planet for more than 130 million years.

Walking on two legs helped the early humans succeed as a species. Their hands and arms were free for handling food and tools. Standing humans were also higher off the ground and better able to see and hear the approach of something dangerous. The size of the human brain helped, too. It is much bigger than a gorilla's or a chimpanzee's.

An adult human's body contains 206 bones. Surprisingly, a newborn baby has many more—about 350 bones! As a baby grows, some bones join together to make larger ones.

The top of the skull is large and round. It holds and protects the big brain. Although most of the skull looks like one big bone, it is made of 22 bones joined tightly together. Special hinges connect the lower jaw to the rest of the skull so the jaw moves easily.

The ribs make a cage which curves around from the backbone to the breastbone. Ribs are strong enough to protect the delicate lungs beneath them but light enough to move in and out as we breathe.

The human backbone is made up of many small bones called vertebrae—just like the backbones of other animals. But the human backbone is a vertical support. In four-legged animals, it is a horizontal support. At the end of the backbone is the coccyx or tail bone. This is all the tail that humans have left.

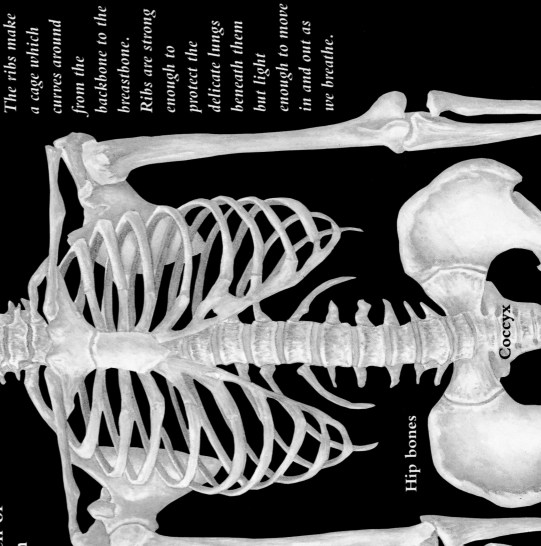

Hip bones

Coccyx

The 27 bones of a human hand make for great flexibility. Fingers and thumb can touch together which helps us grasp even the smallest objects firmly.

The human foot is a flat platform designed for walking—not for gripping branches. Human toes are much shorter than gorilla toes, and our big toe cannot be placed against our other toes. We have 26 bones in each foot.

The thigh bone, or femur, is the largest bone in the human body. The thigh bones are angled so that they place the lower limbs directly under the body's weight. This makes walking on two legs easier.

The hip bones, or pelvis, connect the legs to the torso. Animals that walk mostly on four legs have long pelvises. Humans have a more bowl-shaped pelvis, suited to upright movement on two legs, with the legs placed directly below the torso.

VERSATILE MOVER

Humans cannot run as fast as horses, jump as high as kangaroos, or swim as gracefully as seals. But we do all these things pretty well. While the bodies of many other animals are specialized for a particular way of life, humans are built for a remarkable variety of activity.

GLOSSARY

AMPHIBIAN
An amphibian is a cold-blooded creature with a backbone and soft skin without scales that lives both in water and on land. Most amphibians lay eggs in water. The eggs hatch into swimming fishlike tadpoles. The tadpoles grow and change into adult animals, most of which can live on land. Amphibians include frogs, newts, and salamanders.

CARTILAGE
Tough, elastic material at the ends of bone and often part of the joints between bones. Smooth cartilage in joints helps them move more easily.

FIN
A flap on the body of a fish that pushes against the water when the fish moves. Dorsal fins are on the fish's back; ventral fins are on the belly. Pelvic fins and pectoral fins are both paired—there is one of each on each side of the body. Pectoral fins are just behind the head, and pelvic fins farther back.

FLIPPER
The paddlelike structure on the body of sea-living mammals, such as whales and seals. Flippers are actually the animal's arms and legs changed into a shape more suitable for moving through water. (Some birds, such as penguins, use their wings as flippers.)

GILL
The opening on each side of a fish's head through which it breathes. As water flows into the mouth and out over the gills, the fish absorbs oxygen from the water.

GLAND
A part of the body that produces special substances, such as hormones, enzymes, and poisons, which are passed to the outside of the body or into the blood. A gland in a pit viper, for example, makes the poison that the snake injects into its victim as it bites.

HOOF
The thickened nail at the tip of a toe bone on which an animal walks. Horses have a single hoof on each foot—the tip of the third toe. Cattle have two hooves on each foot— the tips of the third and fourth toes.

KEEL
The large extension of the breastbone to which a bird's powerful flying muscles are attached.

LUNG
A spongy, baglike organ in the chest of most amphibians and all reptiles, birds, and mammals. Air is drawn into the lungs so that the body can absorb oxygen.

MAMMAL
A mammal is a warm-blooded animal with a backbone and a covering of fur or hair. Nearly all female mammals give birth to live young, which they feed with milk from their mammary glands. Mammals include dogs, cats, horses, and humans.

MARSUPIAL
A marsupial is a mammal, but its young are born before they are completely developed. Marsupial babies continue developing in a pouch on the mother's body. Marsupials include kangaroos, wallabies, and opossums.

MUSCLE
A bundle of fleshy fibers attached to bones in the body. The muscles contract—get shorter—to move parts of the body.

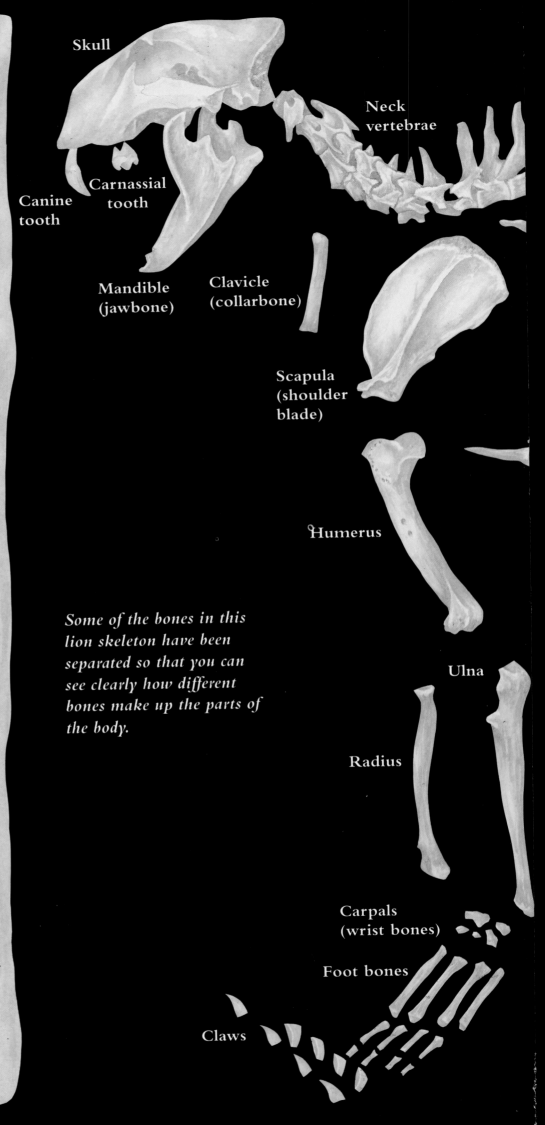

Some of the bones in this lion skeleton have been separated so that you can see clearly how different bones make up the parts of the body.

Skull

Neck vertebrae

Carnassial tooth

Canine tooth

Mandible (jawbone)

Clavicle (collarbone)

Scapula (shoulder blade)

Humerus

Ulna

Radius

Carpals (wrist bones)

Foot bones

Claws

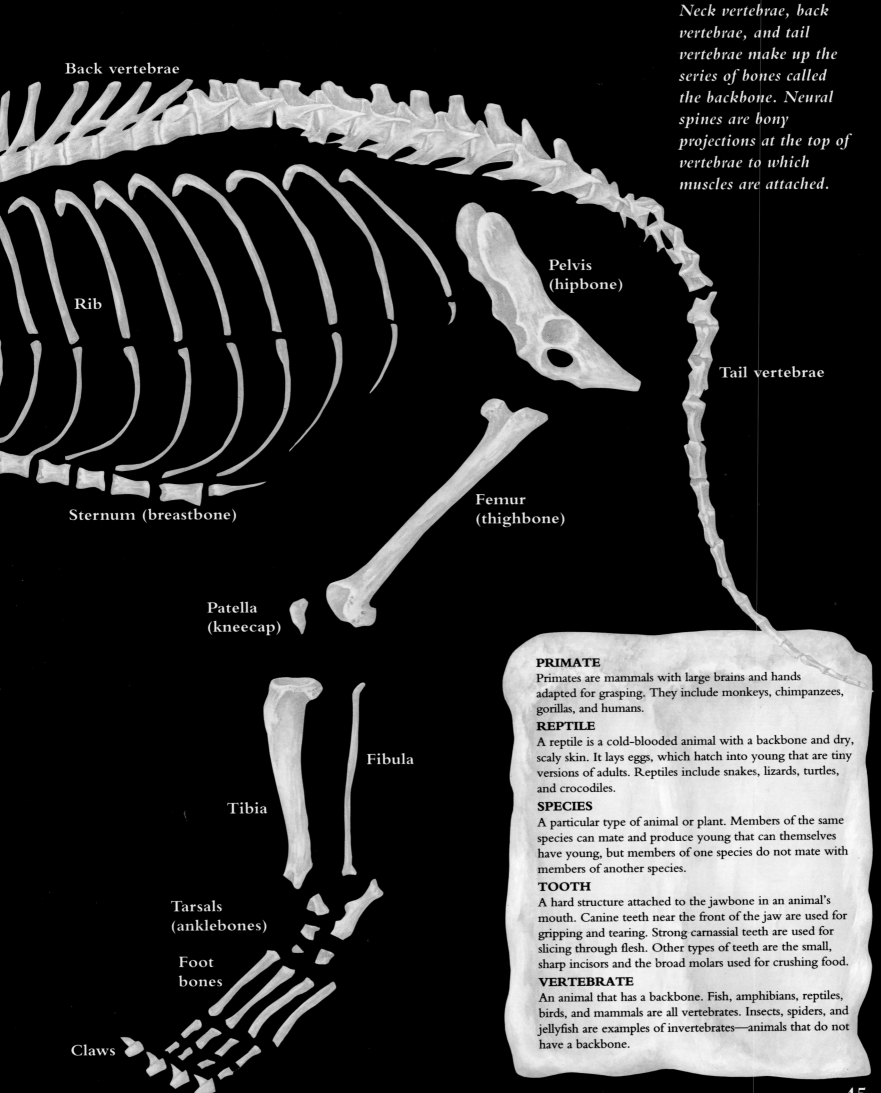

Back vertebrae

Rib

Sternum (breastbone)

Pelvis
(hipbone)

Femur
(thighbone)

Tail vertebrae

*Neck vertebrae, back
vertebrae, and tail
vertebrae make up the
series of bones called
the backbone. Neural
spines are bony
projections at the top of
vertebrae to which
muscles are attached.*

Patella
(kneecap)

Fibula

Tibia

Tarsals
(anklebones)

Foot
bones

Claws

PRIMATE
Primates are mammals with large brains and hands
adapted for grasping. They include monkeys, chimpanzees,
gorillas, and humans.

REPTILE
A reptile is a cold-blooded animal with a backbone and dry,
scaly skin. It lays eggs, which hatch into young that are tiny
versions of adults. Reptiles include snakes, lizards, turtles,
and crocodiles.

SPECIES
A particular type of animal or plant. Members of the same
species can mate and produce young that can themselves
have young, but members of one species do not mate with
members of another species.

TOOTH
A hard structure attached to the jawbone in an animal's
mouth. Canine teeth near the front of the jaw are used for
gripping and tearing. Strong carnassial teeth are used for
slicing through flesh. Other types of teeth are the small,
sharp incisors and the broad molars used for crushing food.

VERTEBRATE
An animal that has a backbone. Fish, amphibians, reptiles,
birds, and mammals are all vertebrates. Insects, spiders, and
jellyfish are examples of invertebrates—animals that do not
have a backbone.

45

INDEX